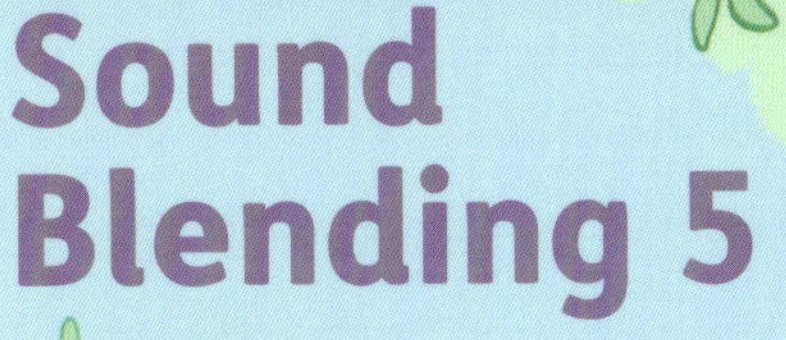

Illustrated by **Emily Fox**

Series developed by **Ruth Miskin**

OXFORD

How to help your child read this book

Your child has been taught to 'blend' sounds (that he or she has previously learnt) to read words.

Ask your child to read the word on the right hand page. (Do not read the word to your child first.) Ask your child to say the sounds and work out the word. If he or she hesitates, ask him or her to say the sounds more quickly and have another go. (If your child has difficulty, please let the teacher know.) Then ask your child to turn the page to check if he or she was right – using the picture to check. Note that where two letters are underlined, the letters make one sound. Repeat with the other words in the book.

Don't make your child struggle too much and praise them when they succeed.

Do it all with patience and love!

Important note

Read stories to your children that are beyond the level they can read for themselves – every evening. They'll only want to become readers if they experience the joy of listening to a range of stories, non-fiction and poetry. Very soon, they will be able to read those books for themselves, as well as listen to them.

bus

bus

zip

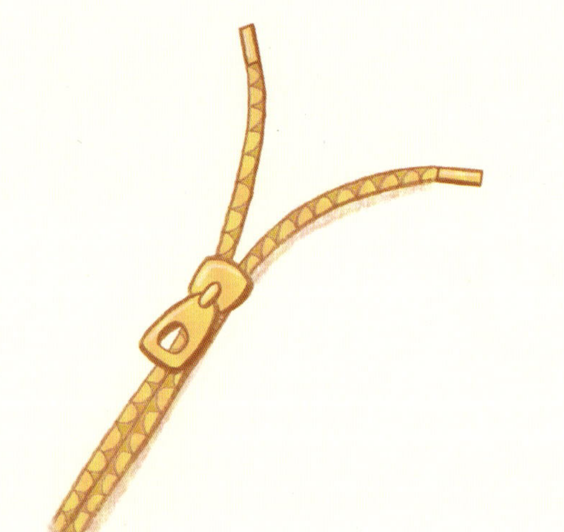

zip

tell

tell

mix

mix

hiss

hiss

hot

hot

till

till

fix

fix

sell

sell

fill

fill

buzz

buzz

well

well

OXFORD
UNIVERSITY PRESS

Great Clarendon Street, Oxford, OX2 6DP, United Kingdom

Oxford University Press is a department of the University of Oxford. It furthers the University's objective of excellence in research, scholarship, and education by publishing worldwide. Oxford is a registered trade mark of Oxford University Press in the UK and in certain other countries.

Mixed Pack of 10
ISBN 9780198437789

Mixed Pack of 100
ISBN 9780198437796

17

Printed in China by Golden Cup

Acknowledgements

Illustrations by Emily Fox

Sound Blending 5

The *Read Write Inc. Phonics* Sound Blending Books provide practice in reading simple words.

Fun pictures support the words, confirming that they have been read correctly.

www.oup.com

web www.oxfordprimary.com
email primary.enquiries@oup.com
tel +44 (0)1536 452610

ISBN 978-0-19-843784-0

9 780198 437840